December, 2010

For Bob & Susan with special
memories of our "happy place".
Love,
Reg & Fred

Outer Banks

on my mind

Cape Hatteras National Seashore KEN TAYLOR

❝ The shore is an ancient world, for as long as there has been an earth and sea, there has been this place of the meeting of land and water. ❞

Rachel Carson

The Globe Pequot Press

Guilford, Connecticut

The best thing about cloudy mornings is that they make for a marvelous sunrise,
like this one over the sea at Pea Island. LAURENCE PARENT

> **"** *The coast is not a place where you can easily ignore the elements. Storms can be seen for miles, advancing like spreading stains. The sea sloshes dark and broody beneath a pastel dawn. . . .* **"**
>
> Jan Deblieu

Whorls of wonder can be found in a simple shark's eye seashell. BILL LEA

Beams of orange shoot onto the sound. ROBB HELFRICK

Stillness prevails at dawn on the Cape Lookout National Seashore. KELLY CULPEPPER

Sea turtles hold a special place in the hearts of Outer Bankers.

"*Nature's show has been the draw for many people who've made the Outer Banks their home. Whether it be stars or clouds, big sky, big fish, or big wind, maritime forest, beach, marsh, or the endless vistas of open water, the show plays year round. Winter is the time when locals claim their seats.*"

Chris Kidder

A leatherback turtle's tracks on the beach are a telltale sign of nesting season. A. BLAKE GARDNER

The Currituck Club, on the National Historic Register, is a landmark hunt club
on the Currituck Outer Banks. KEN TAYLOR

Decoys hang in wait for duck-hunting season on Colington Island. DREW C. WILSON

9

Canada geese enjoy the shallow waters at one of their favorite wintering spots, Lake Mattamuskeet.
LARRY DITTO

" *In that large winter sky, the world turns as it always has but, at first glance, life on the Outer Banks seems to stand still. In this place on the edge of the ocean, where nature so often has her way, it's only fitting that life imitates its nemesis. Summer sizzles, winter chills out. Summer brings a feeding frenzy; winter, hibernation.* "

Chris Kidder

It's a beautiful morning in the marshes, even if the ducks never come. KEN TAYLOR

A good dog waits patiently out of sight.
KEN TAYLOR

Buxton Woods, thick with yaupon, ironwood, and holly, is a 3,000-acre maritime forest in the unlikely location of Hatteras Island. A. BLAKE GARDNER

Gray fox live on the Outer Banks in maritime forests and areas of low, covered shrubs. BILL LEA

This abandoned fishing shack was once a prime location for a happy angler. LAURENCE PARENT

> 66 *The dwellings were built simply, even casually, of readily available materials, including ... wood salvaged from ship-wrecks. Destruction by storms was thus no great loss, and additions and expansions were made almost continuously. . . .* 99

Catherine W. Bishir

A commercial fisherman culls a bluefish from a net on the beach in Kill Devil Hills.
DREW C. WILSON

Marshy Molasses Creek is a well-known waterway on Ocracoke Island. LARRY ULRICH

> " There is no place on
> earth quite like the Outer
> Banks. At the widest point, the
> islands sweep out 20 miles
> into the Atlantic, farther than
> any barrier islands anywhere
> in the world. Narrow shifting
> ribbons of sand, the islands
> are banked on the west by
> sounds and on the east by the
> Atlantic Ocean. "

Jenny Edwards

An adult piping plover, a threatened
species, nests in a carefully chosen
area of vegetated beach. TOM VEZO

Whitewashed Ocracoke Lighthouse is a refreshing site at any hour. A. BLAKE GARDNER

The sun peeks over the lip of the Hatteras horizon, presenting a bounty of colors to those who are up to see them. A. BLAKE GARDNER

" It is only in the seascape of imagination that one can appreciate what lighthouses meant to the blood and bones of mariners in the days before electronic navigation. "

Jenny Edwards

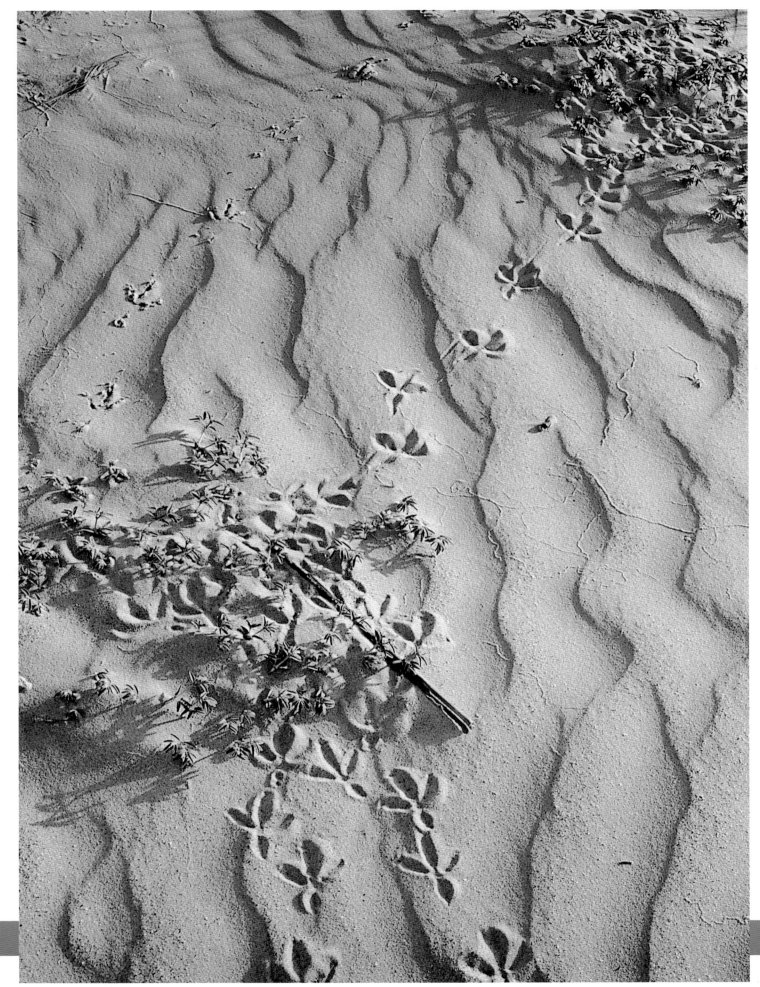

Delicate footprints leave an impression in the wind-whipped dunes. ROBB HELFRICK

Sea oats stand tall and proud as the sun slips into the Pamlico Sound. DOYLE BUSSEY/TRANSPARENCIES INC.

"Among the dunes, tall grasses and waving sea oats compete with pennywort and beach morning glory for a footing in the windblown sands."

David Shears

It's not unusual for beach erosion to reveal the weathered wood of a shipwreck. KIM FENNEMA

Pitcher plants do not naturally occur on the Outer Banks, but they can be seen at the North Carolina Aquarium on Roanoke Island. LARRY DITTO

Delicate, southern blue flag brings another touch of color to the marshes. BILL LEA

A vacation home on a marsh is a great place to start your Outer Banks explorations. ROBB HELFRICK

“*Every September I drive to the Outer Banks of North Carolina, and I know when I'm approaching them because the air smells sweeter, the afternoon sky begins to glow, and I feel an automatic happiness burning into my brain.*”

Mary Chapin Carpenter

Colorful beachfront homes are a coastal attraction unto themselves. ROBB HELFRICK

Well-known Currituck Outer Banker Ernie Bowden shows off a quarter horse. DREW C. WILSON

The beloved wild horses of Currituck Outer Banks roam the land south of Cordova. KEN TAYLOR

DREW C. WILSON

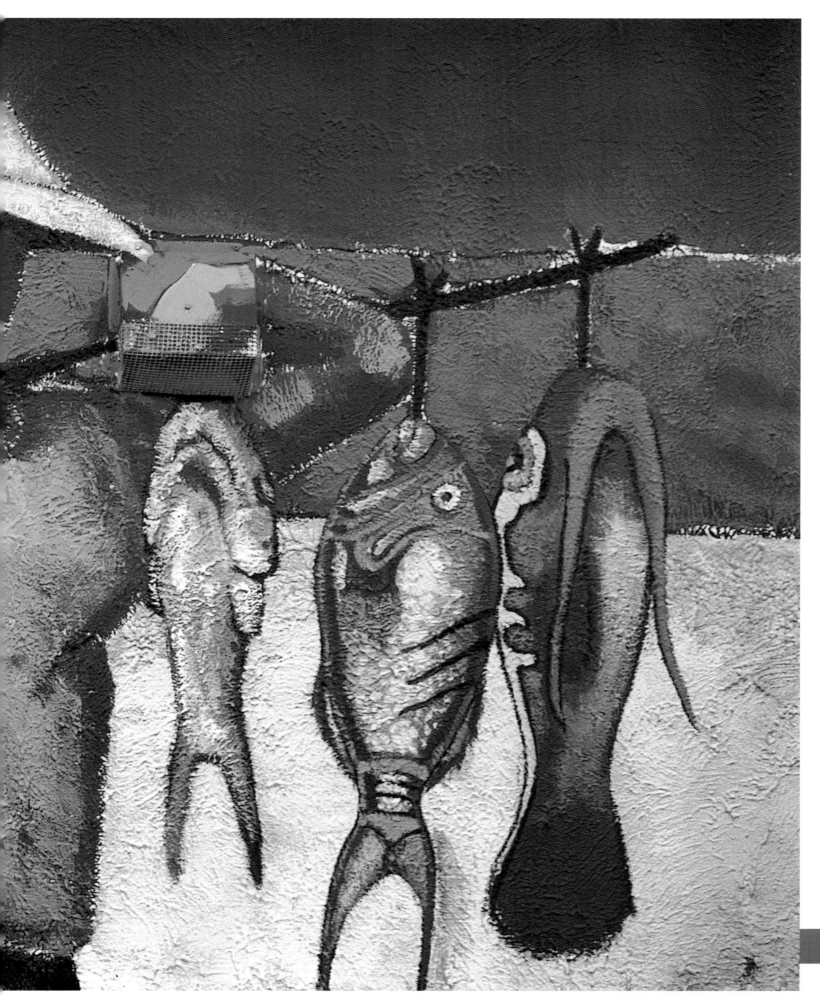

A colorful mural on a popular Kitty Hawk restaurant depicts the island way of life.

Hand-carved decoys are prized reflections of hunting traditions on the Outer Banks. ROBB HELFRICK

Decoy carving requires a precise hand and a careful eye. KELLY CULPEPPER

When skies turn cloudy and gray, seafarers return quickly to harbor. LAURENCE PARENT

Captain Ronald Stowe of the *Captain Squid* is a well-known old salt on Hatteras Island.
TONY ARRUZA

" One learns first of all in beach living the art of shedding; how little one can get along with, not how much. "

Anne Morrow Lindbergh

Beside me the ocean curled its tongue, exhaled in a roar, and admonished me to relax. Someday I will probably discover why the empty shells of razor clams come to the beach all at once, but there is no real rush. This is Hatteras Island, not New York or Nags Head. We are living here, all of us, on island time.

Jan Deblieu

Some days the ocean is so still the locals call it "Lake Atlantic." PAUL REZENDES

Dogwood flowers are signs of spring on Roanoke Island. A. BLAKE GARDNER

Fern fronds catch the morning sun on Roanoke Island. DREW C. WILSON

" It is supposed to be the dying time of year, the drought-sucked moment of Shakespeare's 'sere and yellow leaf.' Instead the grounds of the Elizabethan Gardens in Manteo, N.C., explode in red and green and gold, bird-sung, fountain-splashed, ivy-fastened. The sweet scent of spearmint cuts across wind-crisped herbs like a savory scimitar in a season commonly credited for few flowers or none. "

William Rheulmann

A gangly, but graceful willet prepares for takeoff. TOM VEZO

A majestic, gray-plumed great blue heron wades carefully through an estuary. BILL LEA

Brilliantly feathered wood ducks spend a leisurely winter on the Outer Banks. LARRY DITTO

The old Chicamacomico Lifesaving Station in Rodanthe, now a museum, wears the weathered cedar shakes of traditional Outer Banks architecture. A. BLAKE GARDNER

The Whalehead Club, known as Corolla Island when it was built in 1925, has now been restored to its former glory. LAURENCE PARENT

The laughing gull's loud, high-pitched call gives it its happy name. KEN TAYLOR

Double-crested cormorants swim about with their periscope-like necks above the water. BILL LEA

Small green herons frequent the ponds and ditches at Pea Island National Wildlife Refuge. BILL LEA

❝ The miracle of rebirth comes every day to the marshes as wildfowl stir to the day's endeavors. The long-legged cranes and egrets step their careful way through the shallow waters, and pelicans swoop in graceful flight above the water's surface, each seeking in its own way the sustenance those waters hold. ❞

Walter Cronkite

Commercial fishing boats help bring in the day's catch. ROBB HELFRICK

A bountiful harvest of blue crabs.

Getting to Ocracoke Island is almost as much fun as being there. KELLY CULPEPPER/TRANSPARENCIES INC.

Seagulls follow the ferries looking for a free meal. JANE FAIRCLOTH/TRANSPARENCIES INC.

It's bumper to bumper on the Ocracoke Ferry summer runs. JANE FAIRCLOTH/TRANSPARENCIES INC.

Military history comes alive at nearby Fort Macon State Park. KEN TAYLOR

The view to the sea from Fort Macon can be serenely beautiful.
KEN TAYLOR

Travel through these time-worn passages for a look at the area's history. ROBB HELFRICK

Marsh grasses and the Currituck Beach Lighthouse take on a warm glow in the afternoon sun. LAURENCE PARENT

Finding a quiet nook in a salt marsh is a special Outer Banks experience.
LAURENCE PARENT

Verdant patterns of vegetation adorn Small Pond at Pea Island National Wildlife Refuge. PAUL REZENDES

" The marshes have a beauty of their own that only the
boatman can experience. The tall saw grass that seems to wilt
under the blazing noonday sun glories in the dawn. It reaches
for the rising day, speckled by dew that catches the first light
and, vaporizing, tinges the morning with a delicate mist. "

Walter Cronkite

Trails behind the Bodie Island Lighthouse lead along marshy creeksides abundant with native flora.
LAURENCE PARENT

❝The very thought of lighthouses on the part of North Carolinians is apt to carry a feeling of solidity and permanence. . . . ❞

David Stick

Cape Hatteras Lighthouse, with its signature black and white candy stripes, is a revered symbol of the Outer Banks. HARDIE TRUSDALE

Marinas provide safe harbor for boats all along the Outer Banks. ROBB HELFRICK

A mate unloads a good day's catch
at the docks. DEAN ABRAMSON

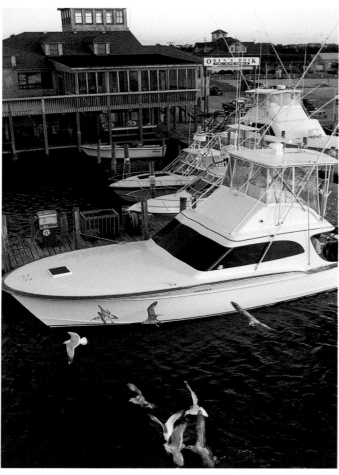

Off-shore sport fishing is big business in Hatteras Village. TONY ARRUZA

" Islands convey a subtle enchantment and Ocracoke casts its own unique spell. It is a place of unspoiled beauty peopled by a special breed of islanders whose distinctive character stems from centuries of isolation. "

David Shears

Smiling anglers show off a rare sailfish catch at Avalon Fishing Pier in Kill Devil Hills. DREW C. WILSON

It's hard to come to the beach and not encounter a flock of laughing gulls. SCOTT SMITH

> 66 *The sight of a flock of avocets, a plentiful but sometimes secretive wader, always makes me feel as if I have been handed a gift. Seeing a true rarity—say, a curlew sandpiper or a swallow-tailed kite—elicits a deep rush of gratitude.* 99
>
> Jan Deblieu

A bright red bill gives the American oystercatcher its distinctive look.
TOM VEZO

Getting on the watch is an essential part of a visit to the Outer Banks. DREW C. WILSON

❝ Wind is culture and heritage on the Outer Banks; wind shapes earth, plant, animal, human. It toughens us. It moves mountains of sand as we watch. It makes it difficult to sleepwalk through life. ❞

Jan Deblieu

With more than 420 acres of sand dunes, Jockey's Ridge State Park is the perfect place to test your wings. JANE FAIRCLOTH/TRANSPARENCIES INC.

Wide, shallow sounds and constant wind make the Outer Banks a windsurfer's paradise. MIKE BODHER

An egret displays its wispy plumage in breeding season. BILL LEA

Alligator River National Wildlife Refuge houses a small population. BILL LEA

A rare albino nutria washes up in the waters of the Pamlico Sound.
LARRY DITTO

" . . . on the North Carolina Outer Banks, the days cannot be defined without wind. "

Jan Deblieu

A replica of the Wright Brothers plane is on display at the Wright Brothers National Memorial Exhibit Center.
LARRY DITTO

The Wright Brothers National memorial in Kill Devil Hills is a majestic commemoration of Wilbur and Orville Wright's first flight on this exact spot on December 17, 1903. LAURENCE PARENT

Ocracoke Lighthouse, built in 1823, is the oldest lighthouse structure on the Outer Banks—and it's still in operation. SCOTT SMITH

Pure in its unpainted red-brick attire, the Currituck Beach Lighthouse stands guard over old Corolla Village.

The sun greets the day in an inspiring way on the Outer Banks. LARRY ULRICH

Coquina Beach's wide, uncrowded stretches are a favorite with Outer Bankers seeking solitude.
LAURENCE PARENT

This part of Carolina is faced with a chain of sand-banks, which defends it from the violence and insults of the Atlantic Ocean; by which barrier, a vast sound is hemmed in, which fronts the mouths of the navigable and pleasant rivers of this fertile country, and into which they disgorge themselves.

John Lawson

Old seafarers find their final rest in the safe harbor of Wanchese Village. DEAN ABRAMSON

Golf and seafood are local pastimes. ROBB HELFRICK

A forgotten wooden skiff succumbs to the elements. ROBB HELFRICK

" *For every mile there is a wreck, for every wreck a deed of heroism, and for every deed a dozen enchanting stories.* "

Bill Sharpe

" Island living has been a lens through which to examine my own life. . . . Little by little one's holiday vision tends to fade. I must remember to see with island eyes. The shells will remind me; they must be my island eyes. "

Anne Morrow Lindbergh

Fresh seafood is guaranteed on the Outer Banks. DREW C. WILSON

Pamlico Sound sunsets have a way of bringing everything to a standstill. KELLY CULPEPPER/TRANSPARENCIES INC.

Young, fit lifeguards watch over the beaches all summer long. DREW C. WILSON

> *" The morning swim has the nature of a blessing to me, a baptism, a rebirth to the beauty and wonder of the world. "*
>
> Anne Morrow Lindbergh

Bliss is a day at the beach. JANE FAIRCLOTH/TRANSCONTINENTAL INC.

Spend a slow day staring out to sea. MIKE BOOHER

A good tousling and tossing in the ocean waves brings out the color and character of seashells.
A. BLAKE GARDNER

Scotch bonnet, found mostly on the southern Outer Banks, is the state shell of North Carolina. KIM FENNEMA

One cannot collect all the beautiful shells on the beach. One can collect only a few, and they are more beautiful if they are few.

Anne Morrow Lindbergh

Commercial shrimping vessels take a break for the day. ROBB HELFRICK

If necessity is in fact the mother of invention, then it is no surprise that Roanoke Island boatbuilders have built up a tradition of fine craftsmanship, taking the raw materials around them to fashion boats uniquely suited to the shallow waters of the sound.

Angel Ellis Khoury

A fishing trawler and skiff in Silver Lake reveal the heritage of Ocracoke Island. KIM FENNEMA

Crab pots are a useful tool in bringing the delicious crustaceans to the table. ROBB HELFRICK

A nature-lover's nirvana, Pea Island National Wildlife Refuge has nearly 5,000 acres of protected wildlife habitat. HARDIE TRUESDALE

" As day visitors today enjoy the stunning natural beauty of Cape Lookout National Seashore, we would do well to remember that while these islands harbor no grudges, neither do these fickle islands hold lasting friendships. They are nature at its wildest, best loved as a romantic fling—an escape, however brief, from the world these barrier islands hold at bay. "

Michael E.C. Gery

Wavelets of sand form in the wind on Jockey's Ridge State Park. ROBB HELFRICK

Mother Nature's artistry—here, sea rocket on sand dune—is evident all over
uninhabited Cape Lookout National Seashore. A. BLAKE GARDNER

Sand surfing is a thrill at Jockey's Ridge State Park, the largest sand dune on the East Coast.
DREW C. WILSON

" At first the tired body takes over completely. As on shipboard, one descends into a deck-chair apathy. One is forced against one's mind, against all tidy resolutions, back into the primeval rhythms of the seashore. Rollers on the beach, wind in the pines, the slow flapping of herons across sand dunes, drown out the hectic rhythms of city and suburb, timetables, and schedules. One falls under their spell, relaxes, stretches out prone. One becomes, in fact, like the element on which one lies, flatttened by the sea; bare, open, empty as the beach, erased by today's tides of all yesterday's scribblings. "

Anne Morrow Lindbergh

Caught in the curl of a Cape Hatteras wave. TONY ARRUZA

The Baltimore oriole, or Northern oriole, is one of 365 bird species commonly seen at Pea Island National Wildlife Refuge.
PHOTOGRAPHER

A rare sighting of snow bunting on a sand fence. TOM VEZO

Cape Lookout Lighthouse, distinctive with its black-and-white diamonds, stands on Cove Banks, on the southernmost portion of the Outer Banks. A. BLAKE GARDNER

Set almost a half-mile back from the ocean, Bodie Island Lighthouse reigns over the marshlands of Roanoke Sound. A. BLAKE GARDNER

Blue crabs are a favorite local delicacy. ROBB HELFRICK

"Creeks rich with ribbed mussels and oysters divide the marshlands into a jigsaw puzzle as they wind into the shallow waters of the tidal flats, where hermit crabs, disguised in the shells of whelks and moonshells, scurry about."

Pat Garber

Skittish ghost crabs blend eerily into the color of the sand. BILL LEA

Channel whelks provide natural decoration for a fence. KELLY CULPEPPER/TRANSPARENCIES INC.

For off-the-beaten-path fly fishing, anglers head to the shallows of freshwater Currituck Sound. LARRY DITTO

Drum must be biting at the Point. GERRY BROOME

Freshwater fishing in beautiful Lake Mattamuskeet offers up a largemouth bass. LARRY DITTO

A semipalmated plover, seen on the Outer Banks almost year-round, finds a resting spot. TOM VEZO

Sweet little sanderlings, dressed in their winter plumage, gather at the shoreline. TOM VEZO

Black-bellied plovers spend their winter eating crabs and sandworms along the Atlantic Coast. TOM VEZO

Shorebirds, like these sanderlings, are very active near the beaches. TOM VEZO

Off-shore wind kicks up frothy surf on Hatteras Island. LAURENCE PARENT